MY FIRST
★★★
MAGIC
B·O·O·K

LAWRENCE LEYTON

DORLING KINDERSLEY
London • New York • Stuttgart

DK

A Dorling Kindersley Book

Designer Mandy Earey

Project Editor Dawn Sirett

Photography David King

Production Paola Fagherazzi

Managing Editor Jane Yorke

Managing Art Editor Chris Scollen

First published in Great Britain in 1993
by Dorling Kindersley Limited,
9 Henrietta Street, London WC2E 8PS
Reprinted 1994, 1995

Copyright © 1993 Dorling Kindersley Limited, London

A CIP catalogue record for this book is
available from the British Library.

ISBN 0-7513-5054-0

Colour reproduction by Colourscan, Singapore
Printed and bound in Italy by L.E.G.O.

Dorling Kindersley would like to thank the following for
their help in producing this book: Christopher Branfield,
Ursula V.L. Branfield, Jonathan Buckley, Helen Drew,
Shelagh Gibson, and Cheryl Telfer. Dorling Kindersley would
also like to give special thanks to the following for appearing in
this book: Oliver Barber, Laura Cole, Martin Cooles, Ebru Djemal,
Natalie Lyon, Julian Morris, Keat Ng, Charles Ocansey,
Chloe O'Connor, Timothy Suckling, and Stacie Terry.

Illustrations by Brian Delf

CONTENTS

MAGIC BY PICTURES

My First Magic Book shows you how to make and perform amazing magic tricks and how to present a magic show in your own home using the tricks you have learned. The magic props are made from everyday materials. Step-by-step photographs and simple instructions tell you exactly what to do, while speech boxes suggest the "patter" (what you can say to the audience). On the opposite page is a list of things to remember when using this book, and below are the points to look for on each page when making and performing the tricks.

How to use this book

The things you need
The things to collect for each magic trick are shown life-size to help you check that you have everything you need.

Equipment
Illustrated checklists show you the tools you will need to have ready before you start to make a magic prop.

Blue "making" boxes
Step-by-step photographs in blue boxes show you how to make the magic props. Clear instructions tell you what to do.

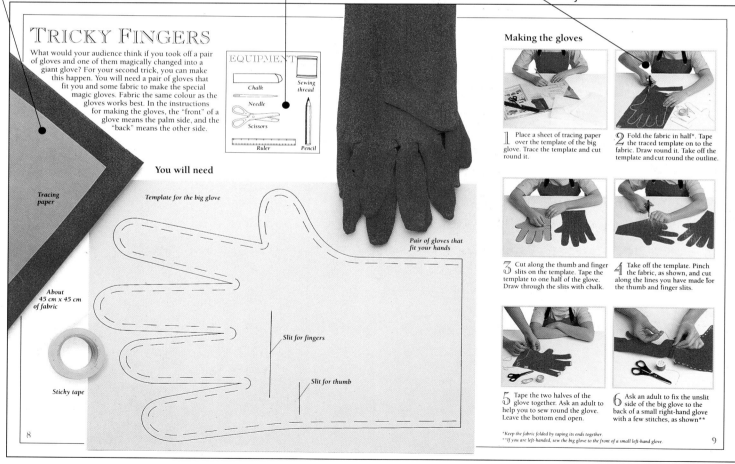

TRICKY FINGERS

What would your audience think if you took off a pair of gloves and one of them magically changed into a giant glove? For your second trick, you can make this happen. You will need a pair of gloves that fit you and some fabric to make the special magic gloves. Fabric the same colour as the gloves works best. In the instructions for making the gloves, the "front" of a glove means the palm side, and the "back" means the other side.

EQUIPMENT
- Chalk
- Sewing thread
- Needle
- Scissors
- Ruler
- Pencil

You will need

Tracing paper

Template for the big glove

About 45 cm x 45 cm of fabric

Sticky tape

Slit for fingers

Slit for thumb

Pair of gloves that fit your hands

Making the gloves

1 Place a sheet of tracing paper over the template of the big glove. Trace the template and cut round it.

2 Fold the fabric in half*. Tape the traced template on to the fabric. Draw round it. Take off the template and cut round the outline.

3 Cut along the thumb and finger slits on the template. Tape the template to one half of the glove. Draw through the slits with chalk.

4 Take off the template. Pinch the fabric, as shown, and cut along the lines you have made for the thumb and finger slits.

5 Tape the two halves of the glove together. Ask an adult to help you to sew round the glove. Leave the bottom end open.

6 Ask an adult to fix the unslit side of the big glove to the back of a small right-hand glove with a few stitches, as shown**

Keep the fabric folded by taping its ends together.
**If you are left-handed, sew the big glove to the front of a small left-hand glove.*

8

9

4

Things to remember

1 Read through all the instructions before you begin to make a prop or perform a trick, and gather together everything you will need.

2 Wear an apron when you are using glue, paint, or glitter.

3 Be very careful when using scissors and sharp knives. **Do not use them unless there is an adult there to help you.**

4 You must use black materials when they are shown for a prop. If you don't use black, it will be harder to fool your audience with the prop.

5 Make sure any paint or glue is completely dry before you use your magic props.

6 Put everything away when you have finished and clean up any mess.

Red "preparation" boxes
Things that you must do before you perform a trick, such as how to put on the magic gloves, are shown in red boxes.

Purple "performance" boxes
Things that you must do secretly during the performance of a trick, that the audience doesn't notice, are shown in purple boxes.

Performance steps
Step-by-step photographs and clear instructions show you how to perform a trick. Speech boxes suggest the "patter" (what to say).

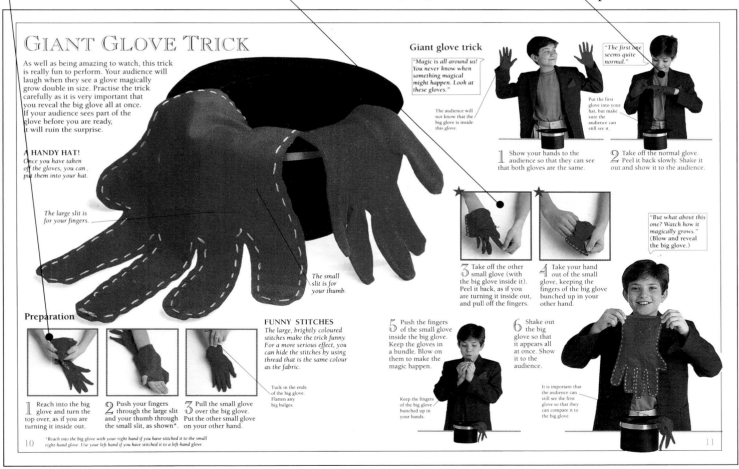

GIANT GLOVE TRICK

As well as being amazing to watch, this trick is really fun to perform. Your audience will laugh when they see a glove magically grow double in size. Practise the trick carefully as it is very important that you reveal the big glove all at once. If your audience sees part of the glove before you are ready, it will ruin the surprise.

A HANDY HAT!
Once you have taken off the gloves, you can put them into your hat.

The large slit is for your fingers.

The small slit is for your thumb.

Preparation

1 Reach into the big glove and turn the top over, as if you are turning it inside out.

2 Push your fingers through the large slit and your thumb through the small slit, as shown*.

3 Pull the small glove over the big glove. Put the other small glove on your other hand.

FUNNY STITCHES
The large, brightly coloured stitches make the trick funny. For a more serious effect, you can hide the stitches by using thread that is the same colour as the fabric.

Tuck in the ends of the big glove. Flatten any big bulges.

10 *Reach into the big glove with your right hand if you have stitched it to the small right-hand glove. Use your left hand if you have stitched it to a left-hand glove.

Giant glove trick

"Magic is all around us! You never know when something magical might happen. Look at these gloves."

The audience will not know that the big glove is inside this glove.

"The first one seems quite normal."

Put the first glove into your hat, but make sure the audience can still see it.

1 Show your hands to the audience so that they can see that both gloves are the same.

2 Take off the normal glove. Peel it back slowly. Shake it out and show it to the audience.

3 Take off the other small glove (with the big glove inside it). Peel it back, as if you are turning it inside out, and pull off the fingers.

4 Take your hand out of the small glove, keeping the fingers of the big glove bunched up in your other hand.

"But what about this one? Watch how it magically grows." (Blow and reveal the big glove.)

5 Push the fingers of the small glove inside the big glove. Keep the gloves in a bundle. Blow on them to make the magic happen.

Keep the fingers of the big glove bunched up in your hands.

6 Shake out the big glove so that it appears all at once. Show it to the audience.

It is important that the audience can still see the first glove so that they can compare it to the big glove.

11

5

MAGIC TOP-HAT

Magicians often wear a special costume. A top-hat with a black tailcoat, gloves, and scarf is a traditional outfit. Here you can find out how to make a top-hat. Worn with a scarf, it will transform your ordinary clothes and instantly make you look the part. You can also use the scarf in an incredible trick. You pull it right through your neck as your amazed audience watches!

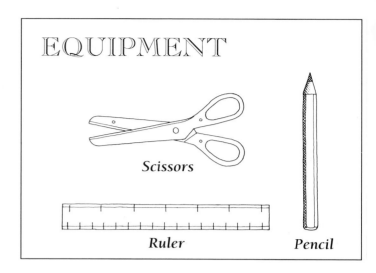
You will need

Glue

Black card*

Ribbon

Long scarf for the scarf trick

Making the top-hat

1 Wrap the card round your head. Ask a friend to mark where the ends meet. Cut it to that length and glue it to make a tube.

Making the brim

3 Draw round the tube on some more card. Draw a 4 cm wide ring outside the circle and a 1 cm wide ring inside. Cut out the brim.

Making the crown

2 Draw round the tube on some card. Draw a 1 cm wide ring around the circle you have made. Cut out and make tabs, as shown.

Finishing off

4 Snip tabs into the inner ring of the brim. Fold up the tabs on the crown and brim. Glue the crown and brim on to the tube.

6

*Enough to wrap round your head and to make a hat that is about 15 cm tall.

The finished top-hat

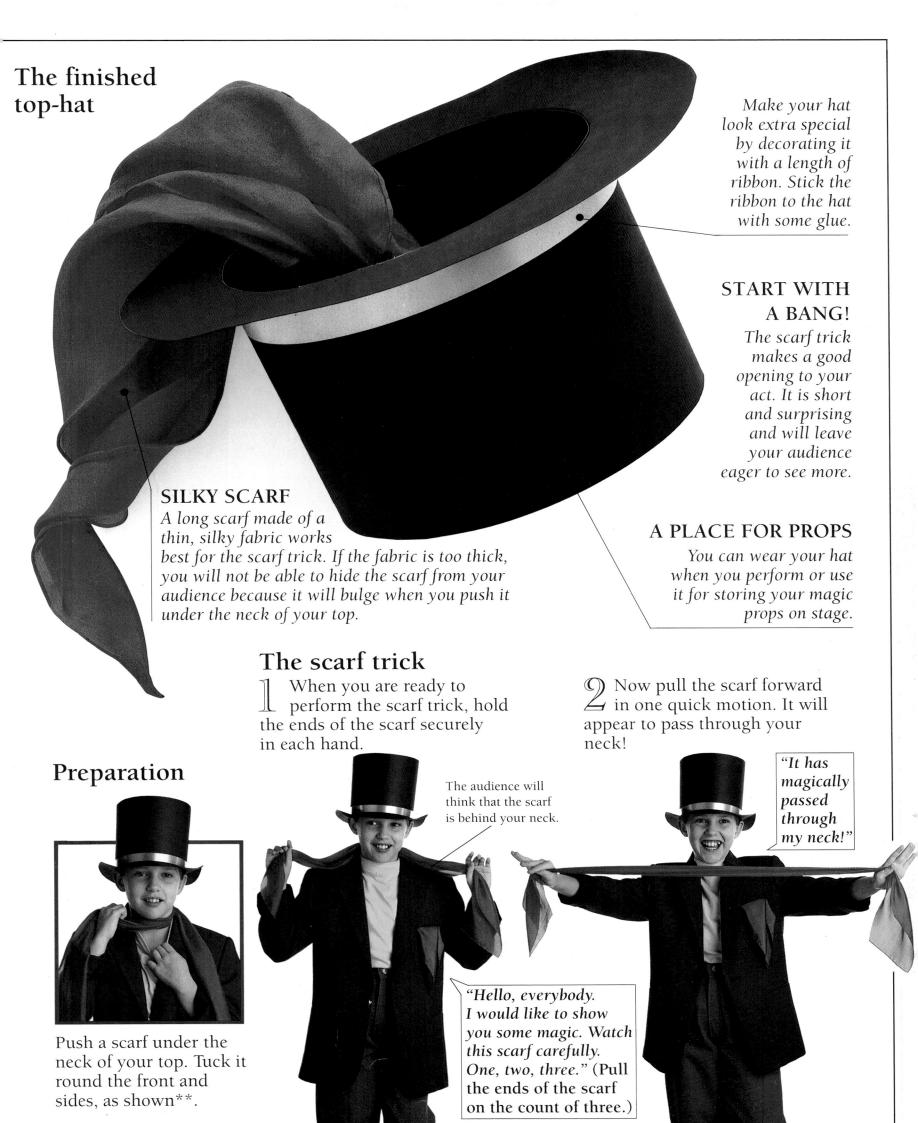

Make your hat look extra special by decorating it with a length of ribbon. Stick the ribbon to the hat with some glue.

START WITH A BANG!
The scarf trick makes a good opening to your act. It is short and surprising and will leave your audience eager to see more.

SILKY SCARF
A long scarf made of a thin, silky fabric works best for the scarf trick. If the fabric is too thick, you will not be able to hide the scarf from your audience because it will bulge when you push it under the neck of your top.

A PLACE FOR PROPS
You can wear your hat when you perform or use it for storing your magic props on stage.

The scarf trick

1 When you are ready to perform the scarf trick, hold the ends of the scarf securely in each hand.

2 Now pull the scarf forward in one quick motion. It will appear to pass through your neck!

Preparation

The audience will think that the scarf is behind your neck.

"It has magically passed through my neck!"

Push a scarf under the neck of your top. Tuck it round the front and sides, as shown**.

"Hello, everybody. I would like to show you some magic. Watch this scarf carefully. One, two, three." (Pull the ends of the scarf on the count of three.)

**Wear a high-necked top for this trick. Do not loop the scarf around your neck.

Tricky Fingers

What would your audience think if you took off a pair of gloves and one of them magically changed into a giant glove? For your second trick, you can make this happen. You will need a pair of gloves that fit you and some fabric to make the special magic gloves. Fabric the same colour as the gloves works best. In the instructions for making the gloves, the "front" of a glove means the palm side, and the "back" means the other side.

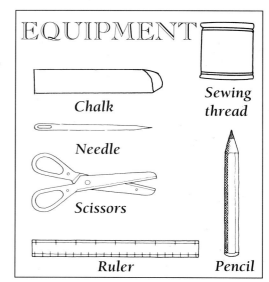

EQUIPMENT

Chalk

Sewing thread

Needle

Scissors

Ruler

Pencil

You will need

Tracing paper

About 45 cm x 45 cm of fabric

Sticky tape

Template for the big glove

Slit for fingers

Slit for thumb

Making the gloves

1 Place a sheet of tracing paper over the template of the big glove. Trace the template and cut round it.

2 Fold the fabric in half*. Tape the traced template on to the fabric. Draw round it. Take off the template and cut round the outline.

3 Cut along the thumb and finger slits on the template. Tape the template to one half of the glove. Draw through the slits with chalk.

4 Take off the template. Pinch the fabric, as shown, and cut along the lines you have made for the thumb and finger slits.

5 Tape the two halves of the glove together. Ask an adult to help you to sew round the glove. Leave the bottom end open.

6 Ask an adult to fix the unslit side of the big glove to the back of a small right-hand glove with a few stitches, as shown**.

*Keep the fabric folded by taping its ends together.
**If you are left-handed, sew the big glove to the front of a small left-hand glove.

Pair of gloves that fit your hands

9

GIANT GLOVE TRICK

As well as being amazing to watch, this trick is really fun to perform. Your audience will laugh when they see a glove magically grow double in size. Practise the trick carefully as it is very important that you reveal the big glove all at once. If your audience sees part of the glove before you are ready, it will ruin the surprise.

A HANDY HAT!
Once you have taken off the gloves, you can put them into your hat.

The large slit is for your fingers.

The small slit is for your thumb.

Preparation

FUNNY STITCHES
The large, brightly coloured stitches make the trick funny. For a more serious effect, you can hide the stitches by using thread that is the same colour as the fabric.

Tuck in the ends of the big glove. Flatten any big bulges.

1 Reach into the big glove and turn the top over, as if you are turning it inside out.

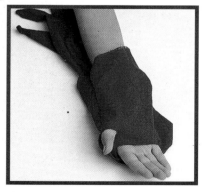

2 Push your fingers through the large slit and your thumb through the small slit, as shown*.

3 Pull the small glove over the big glove. Put the other small glove on your other hand.

*Reach into the big glove with your right hand if you have stitched it to the small right-hand glove. Use your left hand if you have stitched it to a left-hand glove.

Giant glove trick

The audience will not know that the big glove is inside this glove.

"The first one seems quite normal."

Put the first glove into your hat, but make sure the audience can still see it.

1 Show your hands to the audience so that they can see that both gloves are the same.

2 Take off the normal glove. Peel it back slowly. Shake it out and show it to the audience.

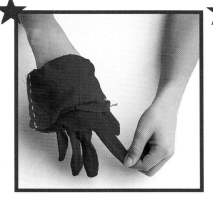

"But what about this one? Watch how it magically grows." (Blow and reveal the big glove.)

3 Take off the other small glove (with the big glove inside it). Peel it back, as if you are turning it inside out, and pull off the fingers.

4 Take your hand out of the small glove, keeping the fingers of the big glove bunched up in your other hand.

5 Push the fingers of the small glove inside the big glove. Keep the gloves in a bundle. Blow on them to make the magic happen.

6 Shake out the big glove so that it appears all at once. Show it to the audience.

Keep the fingers of the big glove bunched up in your hands.

It is important that the audience can still see the first glove so that they can compare it to the big glove.

11

An Eye-catching Tie

Can you imagine wearing a magic tie that is plain one minute and spotty the next? Here you can find out how to make one yourself. You can then baffle your friends and family by making the tie change before their eyes.

This trick works well if you perform it after the Giant Glove trick because it involves another part of your costume. You must use black felt and black paper for the tie. Another colour will not hide what happens in the trick and your audience might guess how the magic tie works. If you turn the page, you can find out how to make a collar to wear with your tie.

Yellow poster paint

Black sticky tape

EQUIPMENT

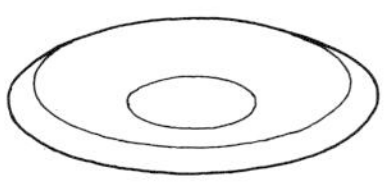

Saucer

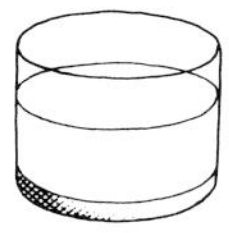

Jar of water

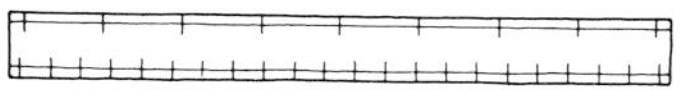

Ruler

Scissors

Paintbrush

Pencils

You will need

Handful of small, yellow paper circles (you can make these by using a hole punch and yellow paper)

About 10 cm of black nylon fabric fastener

About 45 cm x 30 cm of black felt

Yellow card

Thick black paper

Glue

Making the tie

1 Draw a 28 cm x 4 cm rectangle on a piece of thick black paper. Cut it out and cut a curved shape at one end of the rectangle.

2 Fold the black felt in half. Draw a 10 cm line across from the folded edge and a 36 cm line down, as shown. Cut along the two lines.

3 Measure 6 cm across from the fold. Draw a diagonal line from that point, down to a corner. Cut a "V" shape into that end, as shown.

4 Cut along the diagonal line. Unfold the felt. Put the paper in the middle. Draw round it and draw small circles, as shown*.

5 Cut out the circles. Put the paper back on the felt and tape it in place. Turn the felt over. Draw round the holes on to the paper.

6 Take the paper off the felt. Paint yellow stripes on to the paper where you have marked the position of the holes, as shown.

7 Hold the paper on the felt so the stripes and holes don't line up. Fold the paper to make a tab at the straight end. Cut slits in the felt**.

8 Remove the paper. Fold in the sides of the tie and stick them together with strips of tape. Leave the slit open. Glue the end of the tie.

9 Push the paper into the tie through the slit. Leave the tab sticking out. Glue fabric fastener to the tab and tie, as shown.

*The circles should be in rows, about 2.5 cm apart.
**The slits must line up with the fold you make in the paper.

13

SPOTTY TIE TRICK

The yellow and black strip of paper inside the tie holds the secret to this trick. When the fabric fastener is stuck down, the paper is held up and the tie is plain black. But when you flick the fastener up and shake the tie, the paper falls down, the yellow paint is revealed, and the tie becomes spotty. Practise in front of a mirror to make sure your performance is perfect.

The small paper circles that you throw into the air are the finishing touch to the trick. They take the audience's attention away from what you are doing to the tie and make an attractive magical effect.

The collar is fastened at the back with nylon fabric fastener.

The width of the felt here should match the width of the felt on the collar.

Making the collar

1 Draw a 6 cm x about 40 cm rectangle on some card*. Draw a line down the middle of the rectangle, as shown, and cut it out.

2 Fold the card along the middle line and cut out a section, as shown. Glue nylon fabric fastener to the ends of the card.

MAGIC SPOTS

Yellow or white spots or another bright colour show up best against the black tie. You might need to paint two coats of yellow paint to cover the black paper.

3 Cut out a triangle of felt that is a little wider at the top than the section of card you have cut out. Glue it inside the folded card.

4 Glue both sides of the end of the triangle of felt. Push it into the top of the tie, as shown, and press down to make the glue stick.

FINISHING TOUCHES

For a neat finish, ask an adult to iron your tie.

Wrap the card round your neck to find the exact length you will need.

Preparation

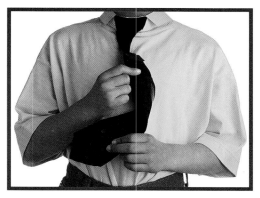

1 Put on the tie. The fabric fastener should be stuck down so that the tie looks plain black from a distance.

2 If you are right-handed, fill your left pocket with small yellow circles. If you are left-handed, fill your right pocket.

The tie trick

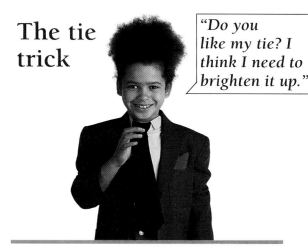

"Do you like my tie? I think I need to brighten it up."

1 Show the audience the plain tie. Hold it at the top, above the paper, so that it doesn't appear stiff**.

"I know, I'll use my magic."

2 While you are getting a handful of paper circles from your pocket, move your other hand down to the fabric fastener.

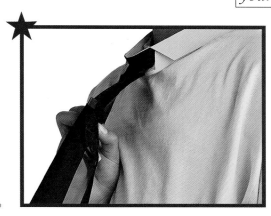

3 While still getting the paper circles, secretly flick up the fabric fastener by using your thumb, as shown.

"Watch, as spots appear before your eyes!"

4 As you throw the paper circles into the air in front of you, move your hand above the nylon fabric fastener and shake the tie.

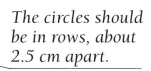

The circles should be in rows, about 2.5 cm apart.

The ends of the tie are glued together to stop the paper strip from falling out. Don't push the paper into the tie until the glue is dry.

"Now, that looks better, doesn't it?"

5 The yellow paint will be revealed as the paper moves down and the tie will look spotty. Show the spotty tie to the audience.

**Use your right hand if you are right-handed and your left hand if you are left-handed.

15

MAGIC WAND

This magic wand is very special. It will rise up on its own through your fingers! Practise using the wand in front of a mirror to make sure that the trick looks natural. A magic wand is also a useful prop to have when you are performing other tricks in your act. You can wave it in the air when you say magic words to make things appear or disappear.

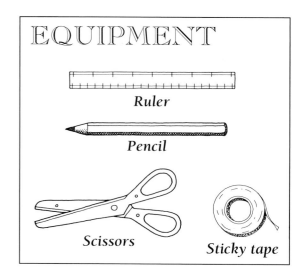
You will need

Two gold buttons

Elastic

Blue and gold paper

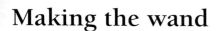

Narrow cardboard sweet tubes (use one long tube or tape two short tubes together)

Gold and silver stars

Glue

Making the wand

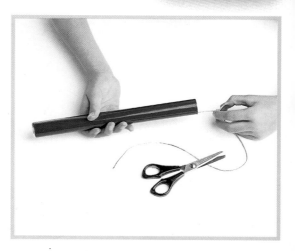

1 Use one long, narrow tube or tape two short, narrow tubes together, as shown. Cover the tube with coloured paper.

2 Tie a button to one end of a length of elastic*. Push the elastic through the tube and glue the button to the end of the tube.

3 Tie a button to the other end of the elastic. The elastic must be taut enough to hold this button in place. Cut off any excess elastic.

The elastic should be a bit longer than the length of the tube you use.

DECORATING THE WAND

Make your wand sparkle with gold and silver stars and gold-coloured paper. Use strong glue to stick the stars and paper in place.

BUTTONS

Buttons that are slightly bigger than the tube work best. You will find them easier to pick up between your thumb and first finger without the audience noticing.

Gold paper for the ends of the wand

Button

Button

Blue paper

Stars for decoration

The magic wand trick

1 Pick up the button that isn't glued to the wand. Pinch it between your thumb and first finger. Practise until you can do this perfectly.

Hold the button between your thumb and first finger.

2 Turn the wand upright and pull the elastic along the side of the wand, as shown.

3 Now make the magic happen by moving your fingers under the wand. Hand movements like these are called "magical passes".

The wand moves up as the elastic is pulled back into the tube.

"To help me with my magic, I'll use my magic wand. It's very special. Watch carefully."

4 Keep moving your fingers under the wand. At the same time, loosen your grip on the wand so that it slowly moves up.

Hold on to the button as you push the wand down.

"You can see that this wand has a life of its own!"

5 To repeat the trick, simply push the wand down with your other hand.

CONJUROR'S CONE

In this trick, you show your audience a silk handkerchief and then place it into a paper cone. As quick as a flash, the handkerchief disappears! Silk handkerchiefs are a popular magic prop. Magicians call them "silks". They are perfect for hiding up your sleeve or in a small space because they are light and squash up small. There are several tricks in this book that use silks. You can perform the tricks using other lightweight fabrics, but silk will give you the best results. If you can, buy a few silk handkerchiefs or cut an old silk scarf into squares.

Making the cone

1 Cut out two squares of thick black paper with sides of 20 cm. Draw three lines on each piece of paper, as shown.

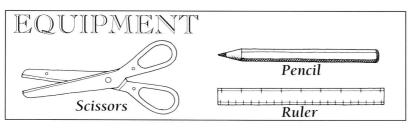

EQUIPMENT

Scissors

Pencil

Ruler

You will need

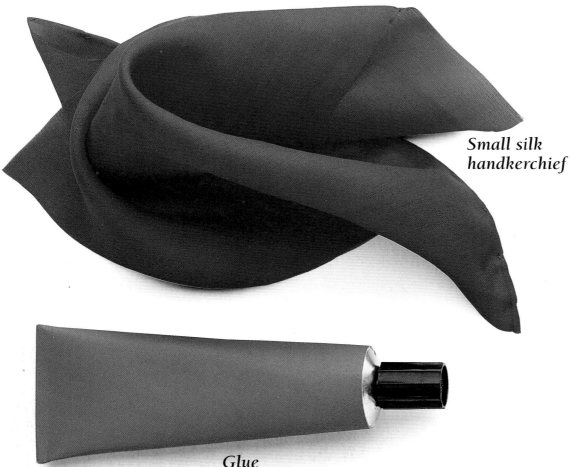

Small silk handkerchief

Glue

Coloured paper for decoration

Thick black paper

2 Put one piece of paper on top of the other. Glue the two squares of paper together up to one of the long lines, as shown.

3 Glue along the edge of the remaining long side. Leave the short side open to make a secret pocket. Fold to make a cone*.

Fold along the two long lines made in step 1.

The finished conjuror's cone

The paper cone trick is one of the simplest ways to make a silk handkerchief vanish, but it is also one of the best. Try to perform the trick very quickly, as the quicker you can do it, the more incredible it appears!

Circles of coloured paper

Fold the side of the cone with the secret pocket under the other side.

DECORATION

Decorate the cone with brightly coloured paper cut-outs. Stick them to the front and back of the cone.

Use a small silk that fits in the secret pocket without showing as a bulge beneath the paper.

Strips of coloured paper

The paper cone trick

"I would like to show you a trick with this cone and a silk."

"Now you see the silk."

1 Unfold the cone and show the audience the front and back of the paper.

2 Fold the paper and make it into a cone. Push the silk into the secret pocket.

"Abracadabra – and now you don't!"

5 Unfold the cone and show the audience the front and back of the paper. The silk has vanished!

3 When you push the silk into the cone, you must really put it into the secret pocket.

4 Now quickly clap the cone together in your hands. This flattens the silk in the secret pocket and also makes the magic happen.

VANISHING SILK

Here you put a silk handkerchief in a clear plastic cup and cover the open end. Under these impossible conditions, you make the silk vanish! The secret to the trick is a piece of equipment called a "pull", which pulls the silk up your sleeve. This pull is made from fishing line, which you can buy from fishing tackle shops.

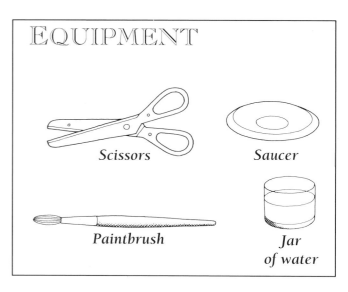

Scissors   *Saucer*

Paintbrush   *Jar of water*

You will need

About 2 m of 20 lb (9 kg) nylon fishing line

Poster paints

Glue

5 cm of nylon fabric fastener

Sticky tape

Sewing binding (enough to fit around your wrist)

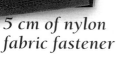

Clear plastic cup

Orange silk handkerchief

Making the pull

1 Glue the nylon fabric fastener on to each end of the piece of binding. Wrap tape round the middle of the binding, as shown.

2 Tie one end of the fishing line securely around the tape*. (The tape will hold the fishing line in place on the wristband.)

3 Fasten the wristband to your wrist and wrap the line round your back, holding it with your other hand.

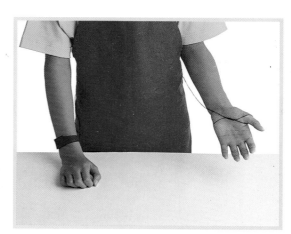

4 Cut the line to a length that feels fairly taut, but lets your arms hang normally. Make a loop at the end to fit over your thumb.

20

*We have used black thread so that you can see clearly how to make and use the pull. You should use fishing line.

The pull

You will probably need to test out your pull a few times to make sure it is the right length. It should be long enough to let your arms hang normally, but short enough to pull the silk right up your sleeve at lightning speed.

Orange silk handkerchief

Decorate your cup by painting a pattern around the rim.

Wristband

Nylon fishing line

WRISTBAND

If you can't find nylon fabric fastener, you can use a thick elastic band for the wristband.

Find out if you can do the trick better with the loop on your left or right hand. Wear it on the hand that you prefer.

Preparation

Attach the band to your wrist and hook the loop over your thumb. Then put on a jacket.

Vanishing silk trick

"For this trick, I need a silk and a cup. Would you like to examine the cup?"

1 Show the audience the silk and then give them the cup so that they can examine it.

2 Secretly, push the silk into the loop, holding the loop open, as shown**.

"I shall cover the open end. Now don't take your eyes off the silk."

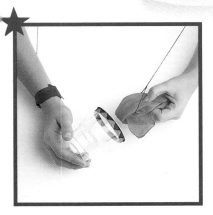

3 Slip the loop off your thumb and hold on to the silk.

4 Push the silk, which you have now threaded through the loop, into the plastic cup. Hold the cup between your hands, as shown.

5 Say the magic words and quickly throw the cup into the air with both hands (the silk will be pulled up your sleeve by the fishing line). Catch the cup and show that the silk has vanished.

"Hey-presto! The orange silk vanishes into thin air!"

**You can do steps 2 and 3 while the audience is examining the plastic cup.

21

MAGICAL COLOUR CHANGE

In the last trick, you made an orange silk handkerchief vanish. Here, you take a red and yellow silk and magically blend them together to make a new orange silk. You will need another orange silk for this trick, since the one that vanished in the last trick will stay up your sleeve throughout your performance. This is one of the ways you can develop the Vanishing Silk trick. You will find another way on page 24.

Making the tube

1 Cut out two pieces of black paper (one 21 cm x 21 cm, one 6 cm x 10 cm). Roll and glue the smaller one to make a tube.

2 Put glue on each end of a small piece of ribbon. Stick it securely inside the tube, so that it divides the tube in half.

3 Glue the small tube with the ribbon inside it to one corner of the large piece of paper. Roll up this piece of paper to make a tube.

You will need

Coloured paper for decoration

Glue

Small piece of black ribbon

Small red and yellow silk handkerchiefs

Thick black paper

Large orange silk handkerchief

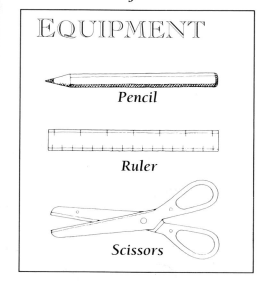

EQUIPMENT

Pencil

Ruler

Scissors

The finished tube

You can cover the outside of the large tube with coloured paper and decorate it with paper cut-outs.

Coloured paper

Zigzags of coloured paper

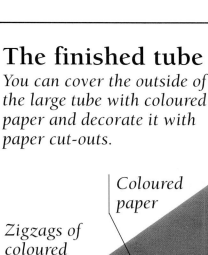

Put the orange silk into this end of the secret inner tube. It will be held in place by the ribbon.

Colour-change trick

"Let's see if I can make another orange silk to replace the one that just vanished. First I'll roll this paper to make a tube."

"Next I'll take a red and yellow silk. Now, what do red and yellow make? Orange, that's right."

The red and yellow silks are on the other side of the ribbon from the orange silk.

1 Unroll the tube and show the audience the front and back of the paper. Keep one hand over the secret inner tube.

2 Roll up the tube. Push the red and yellow silks into the secret tube. (The audience will think they are in the large tube.)

"Now to make the magic happen, I'll blow into this tube. The red and yellow silks have magically mixed together."

"I know what you're thinking – that the silks are still in the tube. But no – the tube is completely empty!"

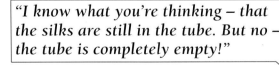

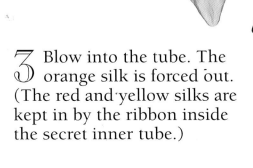

Keep your hand over the secret inner tube, with your fingers together, whenever you show the inside of the large tube.

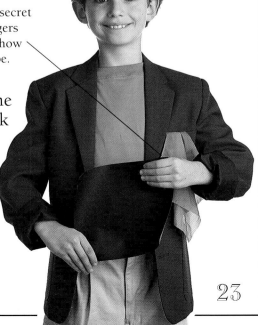

3 Blow into the tube. The orange silk is forced out. (The red and yellow silks are kept in by the ribbon inside the secret inner tube.)

4 Pick up the orange silk and put it in your pocket. Unroll the tube. Show the front and back of the empty tube.

23

SENSATIONAL SILKS

In this trick, you tie together two plain green silks and tuck them into the neck of your shirt. You then take a striped silk and make it disappear. Magically, the striped silk reappears between the two plain green silks! You can make the striped silk vanish by using either the Conjuror's Cone (page 18) or the plastic cup and pull (page 20). Choose your favourite method.

The striped silks are made by colouring plain yellow silks with a felt-tip pen. The ink will bleed a little when you colour the silks. Although slower to use, a thin nibbed felt-tip gives a more accurate result than a thick one.

Two green silk handkerchiefs

Making the striped silks

With a green felt-tip pen and ruler, draw stripes on two yellow silks and colour them in. Draw the first stripe in a corner of each silk.

You will need

Clear plastic cup

Two yellow silk handkerchiefs

Preparation

1 Knot the green corner of one striped silk to a corner of one of the green silks. Roll up the striped silk.

2 Fold and position the striped silk, as shown. Leave the striped silk's green end sticking out from the green silk.

3 Roll up the green silk with the striped silk inside. Leave the green end of the striped silk sticking out.

4 Roll up the other green silk in the same way – from one corner diagonally across to the other.

The three silks trick

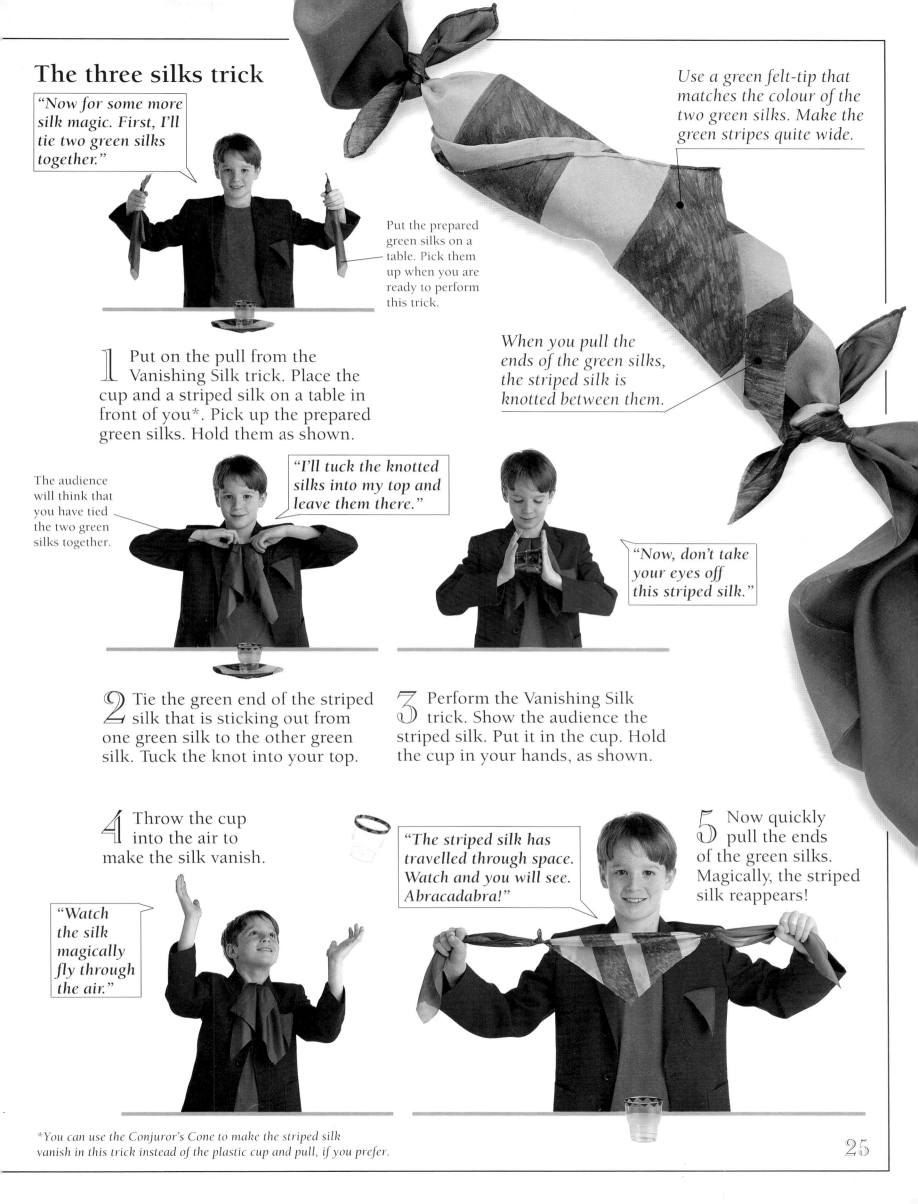

"Now for some more silk magic. First, I'll tie two green silks together."

Put the prepared green silks on a table. Pick them up when you are ready to perform this trick.

Use a green felt-tip that matches the colour of the two green silks. Make the green stripes quite wide.

When you pull the ends of the green silks, the striped silk is knotted between them.

1 Put on the pull from the Vanishing Silk trick. Place the cup and a striped silk on a table in front of you*. Pick up the prepared green silks. Hold them as shown.

The audience will think that you have tied the two green silks together.

"I'll tuck the knotted silks into my top and leave them there."

"Now, don't take your eyes off this striped silk."

2 Tie the green end of the striped silk that is sticking out from one green silk to the other green silk. Tuck the knot into your top.

3 Perform the Vanishing Silk trick. Show the audience the striped silk. Put it in the cup. Hold the cup in your hands, as shown.

4 Throw the cup into the air to make the silk vanish.

"Watch the silk magically fly through the air."

"The striped silk has travelled through space. Watch and you will see. Abracadabra!"

5 Now quickly pull the ends of the green silks. Magically, the striped silk reappears!

*You can use the Conjuror's Cone to make the striped silk vanish in this trick instead of the plastic cup and pull, if you prefer.

DANCING MATCHBOX

Once you have mastered this trick, you will be able to make a matchbox move without touching it. The box will slide across your hand, flip over, and open on its own! Finally, you produce a spider from the box. Practise in front of a mirror to make the trick perfect.

You will need

One empty matchbox

Invisible sewing thread (or extra-fine invisible thread sold in magic shops). Cut a length about 40 cm long.

Safety pin

Two pipe cleaners

Coloured paper

Glue

Making the box

1 Cover the box with paper. Ask an adult to thread a length of invisible thread through the outer box, as shown, and tie a knot*.

2 Tie a safety pin to the other end of the thread. Decorate the box and push the tray into the end with the thread, as shown.

Making the spider

To make the spider's legs, cut one pipe cleaner into four pieces. Wrap another pipe cleaner round the legs to make the body.

*We have used black thread instead of invisible thread to show you how to make and use this prop.

26

The finished box

Decorate the box with a different image at each end. This will help you to find the end of the box that has the thread through it when you are performing the trick.

Small paper star

Spider

Large paper star marking the end of the box with the thread.

LENGTH OF THREAD

You may need to adjust the length of thread. The exact length depends on the distance from your pocket to the position of your hand when you are performing the trick.

Preparation

Put the spider in the box. Pin the thread to the inside of your trouser or jacket pocket and leave the box in your pocket.

The matchbox trick

Make magical passes with your other hand.

"Have you met Zak? Zak is my magic spider! He's in the matchbox. You don't believe me, do you? Watch carefully."

1 While talking to the audience, take the box from your pocket. Put it on the palm of your hand, with the invisible thread running between your fingers, as explained in the next step.

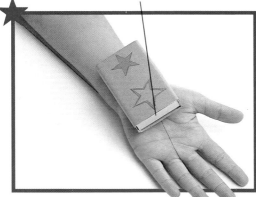

The end of the matchbox with the thread should be here.

2 The thread should run under your forearm and up between your third and fourth fingers. Now, slowly move your hand forward and the box will move forward.

"Zak, turn over and make the matchbox dance!"

Click your fingers as a command.

The thread should now run straight down between your fingers.

3 Turn the box over forwards, so that the side with stars rests on your fingers. Move your hand forward and the box will flip over.

"Now, where are you Zak?"

The thread should be at this end of the box.

4 Turn the flipped box to the side. Bring your hand forward to open the box. Make magical passes with your other hand.

5 Take out the tray and show the spider to the audience.

"Ah, there you are!"

A BAFFLING BOX

Just imagine if you could magically produce a toy rabbit from thin air! You can make this happen by using this magic box. The box consists of three parts, which nest together – an outer square box, an inner tube, and a smaller inner box. The toy rabbit is secretly hidden in the smaller inner box.

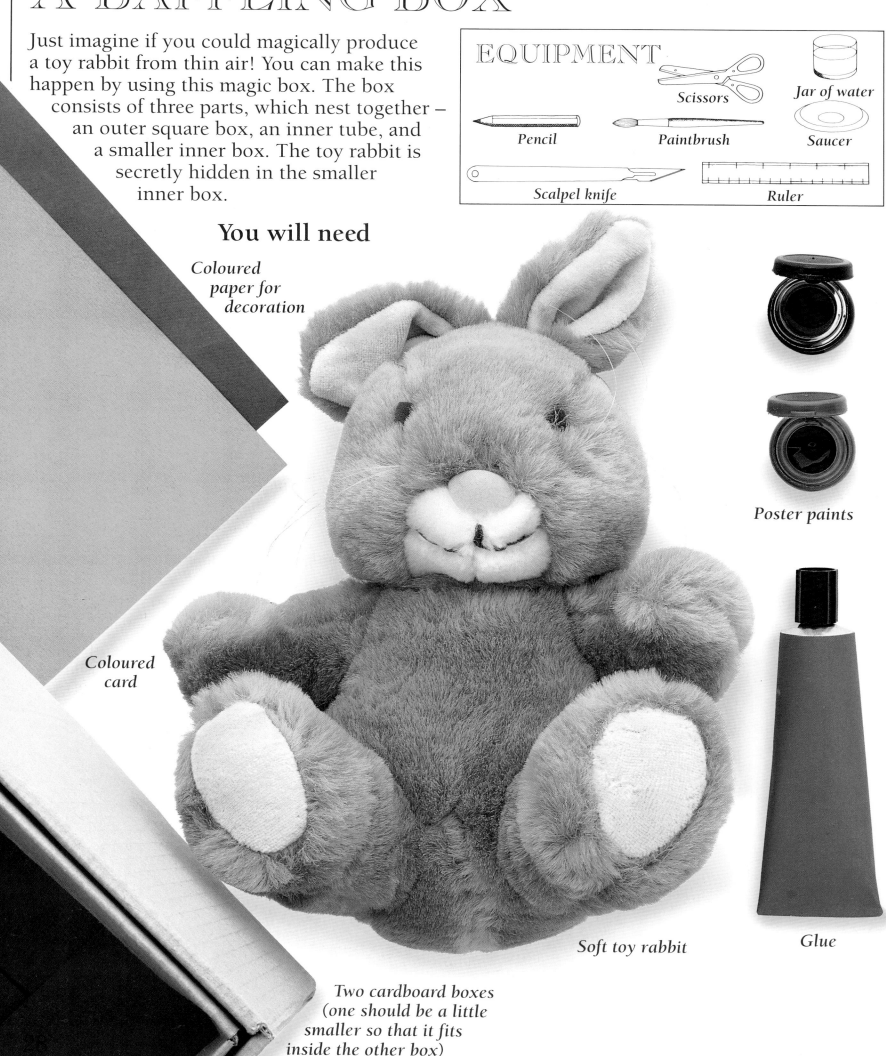

EQUIPMENT

Scissors

Jar of water

Pencil

Paintbrush

Saucer

Scalpel knife

Ruler

You will need

Coloured paper for decoration

Coloured card

Poster paints

Glue

Soft toy rabbit

Two cardboard boxes (one should be a little smaller so that it fits inside the other box)

Making the outer box

1 Cut off the top flaps and the bottom of the large box. Flatten the box, cut it along a fold, and open it out into a long, flat strip.

2 Take the small box and measure its height and width. Write down the measurements you have taken.

3 Draw a rectangle on one side of the large box that is smaller in height and width than the small box. Draw lines across it.

Making the inner tube

4 Ask an adult to cut out long diagonal strips from the patterned rectangle you have drawn, using a scalpel and a ruler.

5 Paint the outside of the box green and the inside of the box black. When the box is dry, glue it back together along the fold.

6 To make the inner tube the correct size, measure the height of the large box. Cut a piece of coloured card to this height.

Making the inner box

7 Place the card into the large box, as shown, to find out how wide you need to make it. It should fit snugly within the box.

8 Cut the card to the width you need and glue on paper shapes for decoration. Glue the ends of the card together to make a tube.

9 Cut off the top and bottom of the small box. Flatten it and cut it along a fold. Paint it black. When dry, glue it back together.

BUNNY IN THE BOX

The baffling box trick relies on the fact that the human eye cannot tell how deep a container is if the inside of that container is painted matt black. When you take out the inner tube, your audience will mistake the front of the secret inner black box for the back of the outer box, and will therefore think that the outer box is empty.

OUT OF THE HAT
Traditionally, magicians have produced live rabbits from top-hats. The baffling box trick is an exciting variation on this theme.

FROM ROSES TO RABBITS
You don't have to conjure up a soft toy. You could produce a bunch of flowers, fruit, balls, a doll – almost anything that will fit inside the inner black box.

PRODUCTIONS
A trick like this is called a "production" because it involves producing something.

Decorate the inner tube with paper stars or moons to make the baffling box look magical.

SETTING UP THE BOX
Make sure that you put the box on a high table, so that the audience looks up at it. If your table is too low, everyone will be able to see the toy rabbit hidden inside the box.

The slots on the outer box reveal the inner yellow tube.

Preparation

Set up the three parts of the prop in this order. Put the toy rabbit in the inner box.

The baffling box trick

"For my next trick, I would like to show you the magic of space. This box is empty."

1 Hold up the outer box and show the audience that it is black inside.

2 Put your hand through the outer box to prove that it is completely empty.

The yellow tube hides the secret inner black box.

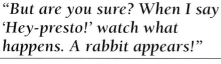

"In fact, as you can see, every space is empty."

The outer green box still looks empty because the secret inner box is painted black.

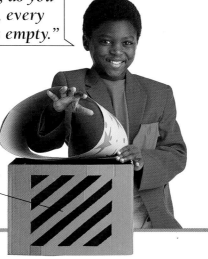

3 Place the outer green and black box back over the inner yellow tube.

4 Pick up the yellow tube and show that it is empty. Then place it back again.

"But are you sure? When I say 'Hey-presto!' watch what happens. A rabbit appears!"

When you produce the rabbit, quickly pull it out of the box and hold it up high. Show it clearly to your audience.

5 Say the magic words or wave your magic wand and produce the toy rabbit from the secret inner black box.

CRAFTY CARDS

Playing cards are used in lots of different magic tricks. Here you can find out how to make your own pack of twenty cards and a special mat, which you can deal on when performing card tricks. Ten of the cards have red spots and ten have blue spots. This is important for the mind-bending card trick that you will find on page 34. A volunteer concentrates very hard and is able to tell you if a card is red or blue without even seeing it.

on page 34

EQUIPMENT

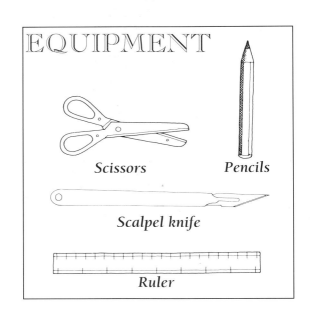

Scissors

Pencils

Scalpel knife

Ruler

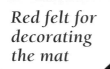

Glue

You will need

Red felt for decorating the mat

Green felt for the mat

Thick black card for the mat

White card for the playing cards

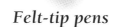

Felt-tip pens

Red and blue circular stickers for the playing cards

The finished cards and mat

It is best to perform card tricks on a cloth or mat, as you may find it hard to pick up playing cards if they are on a shiny, hard surface, such as a table.

Decorate the mat by sticking strips of felt along each edge.

Use this pattern for the back of the playing cards or make up your own.

Ten playing cards have three blue stickers and ten have three red stickers.

Making the cards

1 Colour one side of a large piece of white card yellow. Draw four lines across, 7.5 cm apart, and five lines down, 5 cm apart, as shown.

2 Cut along the lines to make twenty cards that are 7.5 cm x 5 cm. Draw a pattern on the white side of the cards with felt-tip pens.

3 Stick three stickers on to the yellow side of each card, as shown. Make ten cards with red stickers and ten with blue stickers.

Making the mat

1 Draw a square with sides that are 36 cm long on some black card and a square of the same size on green felt. Cut out each square.

2 Spread glue over the card and stick the felt to it. Press down hard to remove any creases and leave it until the glue is dry.

3 When the glue has dried, ask an adult to trim 1 cm off the edge of each side of the mat with a scalpel knife to make a neat finish.

MIND-BENDING CARD TRICK

In this trick, a volunteer appears to know the colour of a card without seeing it! You shuffle your pack of cards and place a red and a blue card face up on the mat to make two rows. You pick out cards and ask the volunteer to say if the cards are red or blue. You then put the cards face down in the chosen row. When all the cards have been placed, you turn them over and find that the volunteer has split the cards into rows of red or blue.

FACE UP OR DOWN
When the cards show their spotty side, they are "face up". When they show their patterned side, they are "face down".

Choosing the cards

"As I pick out cards at random, I want you to think very carefully and tell me if they are red or blue."

"Could I have a volunteer to help me with this trick? Please examine the cards."

Blue card   Red card

1 Ask for a volunteer. Show the volunteer and the rest of the audience the red and blue cards. Then shuffle the pack of cards.

2 Take a red card and a blue card from the pack. Put them face up on the mat, as shown.

Don't let anyone see the cards.

3 Now keep picking out only red cards. Ask the volunteer to say if they are red or blue. Put the cards face down in the chosen row.

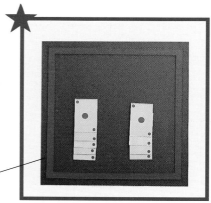

The cards are turned face up here to show you what to do.

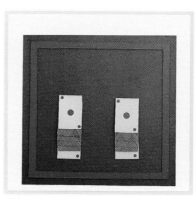

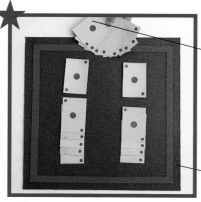

Make sure that the red card in your hand is on the top of the remaining pile.

The cards are turned face up here to show you what to do.

4 The volunteer doesn't know that all the cards you take from your hand are red.

5 When you have two red cards left in your hand, swap the colours of the rows.

6 Use one of the red cards you have left to start the new row. Keep the other in your hand*.

34

*You keep this red card so that you can make a deliberate mistake. This helps the audience to believe in the trick. You can do the trick without the mistake if you don't leave a red card in your hand.

"I'll swap the rows to make it harder. Please look at the remaining cards."

"I'll also put down the cards so that I can't see them. Now, are they red or blue?"

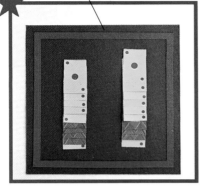

The cards are turned face up here to show you what to do.

Show the red card on top with just two blue cards.

7 Show the remaining cards, but don't let the audience see that all the remaining cards are now blue except for one. Shuffle the cards without anyone seeing them.

8 Put the remaining pile of cards in between the rows, face down, so that you can no longer see the cards when you pick them out. Ask the volunteer if they are red or blue.

9 Continue to pick cards from the remaining pile and to ask if they are red or blue until you have placed all the cards in either row. They will all be blue, except for one.

Picking up the cards

Blue cards   Red cards

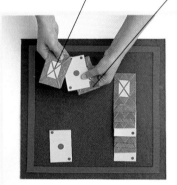

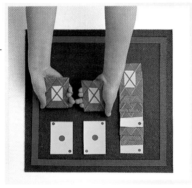

1 Pick up the row that starts with the face-up blue card, as shown. Leave the blue card on the mat.

2 Keep the red cards in your left hand and the blue cards in your right hand, as shown.

3 Put the face-up red card to the left of the blue card. All the cards are now correctly placed for the next step.

4 Turn over the cards in your hands. They will match the colours of the face-up cards on the mat.

Deliberate mistake

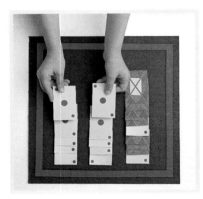

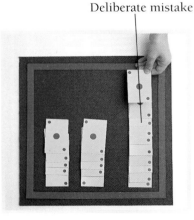

"Now do you believe how amazing the mind is?"

5 Without seeing the cards, the volunteer has put them into rows of red and blue!

6 Now turn over the cards in the other row. The cards will be in sections of red and blue.

7 It will look as if the volunteer knew whether the cards were red or blue and put them in the right rows. There will be one mistake. This helps the audience to believe in the trick.

RING AND ROPE TRICK

Can you make a solid ring pass right through a length of rope, while two people hold on to each end of the rope? This might sound impossible, but it is exactly what you manage to do in this trick. There are two important things that you must learn. The first is how to tie a special knot, and the second is a simple move near the end of the trick, which must be done so fast that your audience doesn't notice it.

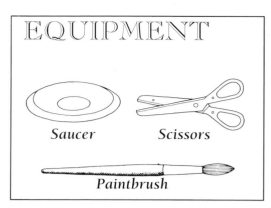

You will need

About 2 m of soft rope

Glitter

Cardboard ring from a roll of sticky tape

Use soft rope for this trick. You will find it difficult to make the knot if you use a length of stiff rope.

Coloured gift ribbon (enough to cover the cardboard ring)

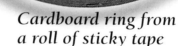

Glue

About 60 cm x 60 cm of fabric

Making the ring

Glue a small section of a cardboard ring. Wrap gift ribbon round the glued section. Keep going until you have covered the ring.

Making the magic cloth

Paint a pattern on a square of fabric with glue. Shake glitter on to the pattern you have made. Shake off any excess glitter*.

*Make sure the glue is dry before you shake off the excess glitter.

36

A magic cloth made out of a shiny fabric looks extra special.

The ring and rope trick

"To do my next trick, I need two people to help me."

"Please hold each end of the rope, while I make the magic happen."

1 Lay the length of rope on a table, as shown. Place the ring over the middle of the length of rope.

2 Ask two spectators to hold the rope, as shown. Cover the ring and rope with the cloth. Tie the knot explained in the next steps.

The pulled section of rope is pushed through this loop.

"It's done. I have now passed the ring through the rope. Please let go of the rope."

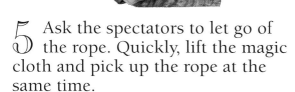

3 Pull a small section of rope through the ring, as shown. Tuck it under the rope to one side of the ring**.

4 Push the pulled section of rope through the loop you have made, as shown. Pull the rope tight to make a knot.

5 Ask the spectators to let go of the rope. Quickly, lift the magic cloth and pick up the rope at the same time.

Pull this end of the rope through the ring.

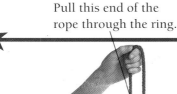

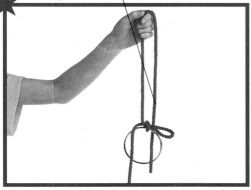

"You don't believe me, do you?" (Pull the rope.) "Now, that's magic!"

Ring

7 Now pull both ends of the rope to undo the knot. The ring will pass through the rope, as shown.

6 As you lift the cloth and rope, quickly pull one end of the rope through the ring. Don't let the audience see this.

**Do steps 3 and 4 under the cloth. We have removed it to show you what to do.

CARD AND COIN MAGIC

In these tricks, you make a card or a coin vanish right before the eyes of your audience! As the tricks are short, you can perform them between other longer tricks to speed up the pace of your act. Both the tricks involve "sleight of hand". This means you make quick, secret hand movements, which the audience doesn't notice. You will need to practise these movements, but the results are worth it. The purple boxes show you the steps that the audience shouldn't notice.

Vanishing the card

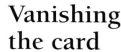
"Watch this card. Now you see it."

HOW TO MOVE YOUR ARM

As you vanish the card, move your arm up and down in a quick motion to hide what you are doing. Lower your arm as you do steps 2, 3, and 4. Raise it on step 5.

1 Take one playing card. Stand side-on to the audience. Show the card. Hold your arm out with the card horizontal between your fingers and thumb, as shown.

Playing cards and coins

2 Bend your second and third fingers behind the card. Move your first and little fingers to each side of the card, as shown.

Overhead view of step 2: You are now holding the card between your thumb and your bent second and third fingers.

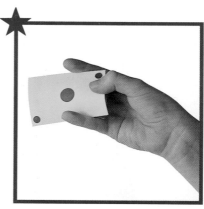

3 Next, clip the card between your first and little fingers, as shown. Your second and third fingers are still bent.

Your second and third fingers push the card round to the back of your hand.

4 Quickly straighten your second and third fingers. They will flip the card round to the back of your hand.

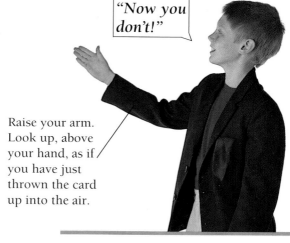

"Now you don't!"

Raise your arm. Look up, above your hand, as if you have just thrown the card up into the air.

5 Now straighten all your fingers. Keep the card clipped between your first and little fingers. Move your arm up as you do this and show your palm.

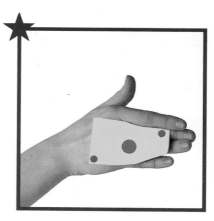

Back view of step 5: The card's edges are now held by your fingers on the back of your hand, as shown.

Reproducing the card

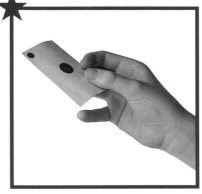

When you reproduce the card, quickly move your arm forward, as if you are grabbing the card out of the air. This will hide the secret movements.

"And as quick as a flash – it's back again!"

1 Quickly bend all of your fingers to bring the card back to the front of your hand.

2 Release the card from your little finger and hold it, as shown.

3 Turn the card upright and hold it between your first finger and thumb.

Vanishing the coin

"Take a good look at this coin."

1 Put a coin on your table for this trick, or borrow a coin from a spectator. Take the coin and hold it between the thumb and first finger of your left hand*.

2 Close the fingers of your right hand round the coin, as shown, as if you are about to take the coin from your left hand.

3 Really, you secretly drop the coin into your left hand, as you can see in this exposed view. Your right hand hides what is happening.

4 Tuck in the fingers of your right hand, as if this hand has the coin. At the same time, tuck in the fingers of your left hand.

"Watch how I squeeze the coin."

The coin is really in this hand.

You use body movements, such as pointing with this hand, to fool the audience. This special skill is called "misdirection".

"Oh, no! It's gone."

7 You can appear to produce another coin by finding one under your arm. (Use the coin that is still in your left hand.)

"Never mind, I'll find another one!"

5 Remove your right hand. You must follow it with your eyes and point to it with your left hand to make the audience think that the coin is in your right hand.

6 Rub the fingers of your right hand together to make the coin vanish. Uncurl your fingers and show the audience that the coin has disappeared.

*If you are left-handed you may prefer to use your right hand here. If you do this, use your right hand whenever the instructions say left and your left hand whenever they say right.

GENIE IN A BOTTLE

In this trick, a genie rises into the air. A trick in which an object is made to float in this way is called a "levitation". Magicians often levitate people. Your audience will be spellbound when they see a genie floating in mid-air! You will need invisible sewing thread for this prop or you can use extra-fine invisible thread, which is sold in magic shops.

You will need

Two beads

Small piece of pipe cleaner

Coloured paper

Clear and coloured sticky tape

Poster paints

Invisible sewing thread

Clear plastic bottle

EQUIPMENT

Ruler   *Scissors*

Saucer   *Jar of water*

Pencil   *Felt-tip pens*

Paintbrush

Scalpel knife

Making the magic genie

1 Ask an adult to cut off the top of a plastic bottle with a scalpel. Paint the base and stick tape round the top and bottom.

2 Cut out a piece of paper that will fit round half of your bottle, as shown. Draw stripes on the paper and put it into the bottle.

3 Draw and paint a genie on some card. Cut out the genie. Glue on beads for eyes and a piece of pipe cleaner for a moustache.

4 Cut a length of invisible thread about 35 cm long*. Fix it to the back of the genie with clear tape in two places, as shown.

*We have used black thread instead of invisible thread to show you how to make and use this prop.

The finished bottle and genie

Your cardboard cut-out doesn't have to be a genie. You could make it an animal, a machine, a monster, a cartoon character, in fact, anything you like. Choose something that suits your act.

The tape covers the sharp edge of the cut plastic bottle, but you can also use it to add decoration. Here yellow and red tape are combined.

Draw the stripes close together. This will help to stop the thread from showing.

Curled pipe cleaner for a moustache

Painted beads for eyes

Preparation

Before your performance, tape the free end of the invisible thread to your chest. Put the genie in your pocket.

"A genie is very special. Make a wish and you'll see what I mean."

2 Show the audience the genie in the bottle. Keep your hand over the bottle so that the top is sealed.

4 Bring the bottle back to your chest to make the genie return to the bottom of the bottle. You can repeat the trick, if you wish. Then turn the bottle upside down and let the genie drop out on to your hand. Put the genie back in your pocket.

We have shown the tape so that you can see how to do the trick. You must hide it. Stick it on one side of your top and wear a jacket. The jacket will hide the tape.

The genie trick

1 Take the genie and put it in the bottle. Hook the thread over your thumb as you place your hand over the bottle.

"Watch closely and keep wishing for something magical. Has the genie heard your wish?"

It will look as if the genie is rising up on its own!

3 Slowly move the bottle away from you. This will tighten the thread and make the genie move upwards in the bottle.

"Look! The genie has heard your wish. Let's hope it comes true. Would anyone like to examine the bottle?"

41

AMAZING MAGIC BOX

Whenever you show your audience this special box, it will look completely empty. But amazingly, when you put your hand into the empty box, you will be able to pull out a dazzling fountain of ribbon and then some brightly coloured sweets. A secret mirror inside the box holds the key to the trick. It makes the box always appear empty. You will need to have a piece of mirror cut to the size given below at a glazier's shop. Be very careful when handling the mirror because the edges may be sharp. Ask an adult to cover them with a strip of clear tape.

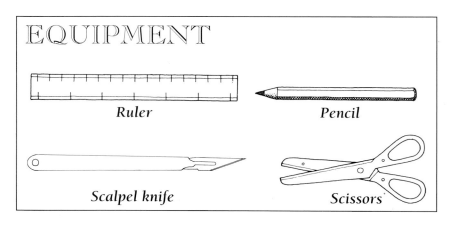
You will need

Glue

Handful of wrapped sweets

Two beads

Mirror (20 cm x 14.5 cm)

Coloured sticky tape for the end of the ribbon

Tissue paper

Striped paper

Coloured card

42

Making the box

1 Draw a box plan on some card. You will need six squares with sides of 15 cm. Draw flaps on three squares, as shown, and cut out.

2 Glue striped paper on to the card*. Make sure you follow the angles of the stripes exactly as shown here.

3 Draw doors on two of the squares, as shown. Ask an adult to cut round them using a scalpel. Fold the doors so that they open.

4 Score the edges of the squares and the flaps with scissors. Fold the card along the scored edges to make a box.

5 Leaving the lid open, glue the rest of the box along the flaps. Fit the mirror inside diagonally, with the reflective side facing down.

6 Close the lid and doors. Glue a bead on to each door to make the handles. You will need strong glue to make the beads stick.

About 10 m of coloured ribbon

*If you can't buy striped paper, you can make your own by drawing stripes on some plain paper.

43

RIBBON FOUNTAIN FINALE

Every performance should have a spectacular finish. This is called the "finale". This trick will make a stunning finale to your magic show. You let the audience see inside an empty box and then produce a seemingly endless length of ribbon from the same box! After showing the box empty again, you go on to produce lots and lots of sweets, which you can throw out to your cheering audience.

PRODUCTIONS

Like the Baffling Box on page 28, this trick is a "production". Productions are good tricks to do at the end of your performance because people can applaud what you produce.

RIBBON

The ribbon makes a colourful display, tumbling out of the box like a fountain. You don't have to use 10 m, but the more you have, the more amazing the trick will appear. When you pull out the ribbon, hold the box up high and tilt it down a little. This will help the ribbon to tumble down on its own, without any help from you.

Instead of wrapped sweets, you could use a handful of colourful beads.

MAGIC STRIPES

When the side door is open, the audience will think that they can see through to the striped back wall of the box and that the box is empty. In fact, the secret mirror is reflecting the striped base of the box. This reflection appears to be the back wall.

MAGIC DOOR

Make sure this door is fairly big. If it is too small, your audience will not be able to see inside the box.

Preparation

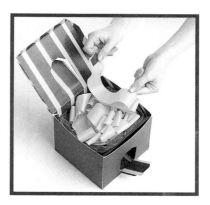

1 Lay some tissue paper on top of the mirror to stop the sweets from rattling against it. Then put in a handful of sweets.

2 Fold the ribbon backwards and forwards into the box, as shown. Fix tape to the end of the ribbon*. Close the lid and doors.

The magic box trick

"Now for my last trick. As you can see, this box is completely empty."

"But, with some magic turns, let's see what we can make."

Whenever you open this door, tilt the box down a little to stop the audience from seeing the mirror.

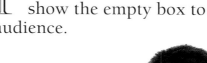

1 Open the side door and show the empty box to the audience.

2 Close the side door. Rotate the box. Turn it to the right and to the left to create the magic.

"The magic has started. The box is now full of ribbon!"

The ribbon will start to tumble down on its own.

"It's empty once more. But wait … Abracadabra! Who would like a sweet?"

3 Open the top door and quickly pull out the taped end of the ribbon. Hold the box up so that the ribbon tumbles down.

*The tape helps you to find the end of the ribbon easily when you are ready to pull the ribbon out.

4 Close the top door. Open the side door and show the audience that the box is empty again. Now close the side door. Repeat the magic turns. Reach into the top door and throw the sweets to the audience.

MY FIRST MAGIC SHOW

Once you can do the tricks in this book, you can link them together and present a show to your family or friends. If there are tricks you can't do very well, leave them out and choose the ones that you are good at instead. Plan your routine and rehearse what you are going to say. You could make up new ways to perform the tricks and different things to say to the audience.

Preparation

Make a list of the props you will need to wear. Check that you have put them on before you perform.

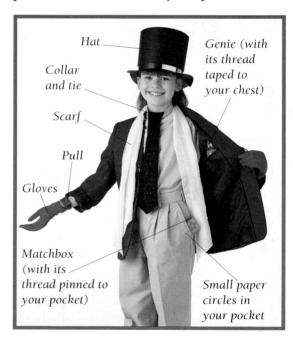

Hat

Collar and tie

Scarf

Pull

Gloves

Genie (with its thread taped to your chest)

Matchbox (with its thread pinned to your pocket)

Small paper circles in your pocket

Performing

Enjoy your performance. Relax and look pleased as you do the tricks. If you are not excited about the magic, your audience won't be either. Save the best trick for the end so that you get a good round of applause.

Speak clearly and don't rush what you say. Involve your audience by asking for volunteers. Don't worry if things go wrong. If you are having fun, your audience will still enjoy your magic show.

Planning an act

A well-planned routine has a good beginning, middle, and end. Short tricks are placed between longer ones to keep up the pace and to hold the audience's interest. You can use the order of the tricks in this book as a basis for your routine, as in the list below:

1 Scarf (page 7)
2 Giant Glove (page 10)
3 Spotty Tie (page 15)
4 Magic Wand (page 17)
5 Conjuror's Cone (page 19)
6 Sensational Silks (page 24)
7 Dancing Matchbox (page 27)

8 Bunny in the Box (page 31)
9 Vanishing Card (page 38)
10 Mind-bending Cards (page 34)
11 Ring and Rope (page 37)
12 Vanishing Coin (page 39)
13 Genie in a Bottle (page 41)
14 Ribbon Fountain Finale (page 45)

AUDIENCE

Keep a short distance between you and the audience. Don't let them sit to the side of you or behind you. Try to seat people in front of where you are going to perform.

COSTUME

Dress up for your show. Your hat, scarf, gloves, and tie will help to make you look the part. Make sure your outfit has some pockets.

BACKDROP

It is a good idea to set up a simple stage for your show. Stand against a backdrop, such as a pair of pulled curtains, or decorate a sheet and hang it up behind you.

MAGIC TABLE

Place a table in front of you. Cover it with a tablecloth or a piece of fabric to make it look special. Lay your magic props in places where you can reach them easily.

MAGIC PROPS

Check your props before you perform to make sure they are in good working order. Prepare props, such as the Sensational Silks and the Baffling Box. When you finish a trick, drop the prop into your hat or on to the floor to make room for the next trick.

MAGIC
TIPS

Practise, practise, practise until
you can do a trick perfectly.

Keep your magic secrets. Never tell
anyone how a trick is done.

Rehearse all tricks in front of a mirror to
see if you are doing them properly.

Choose a performance style that suits your
personality. You can tell jokes or be serious as
you perform your tricks. You can wear
a funny costume or just dress smartly
in ordinary clothes.

If you can, make a video of your
show. Watch it in private to see if
there is anything you need
to improve.

Keep your magic props
in a safe place.